BACKYARD WILDLIFE

Foxes

by Emily Green

BELLWETHER MEDIA • MINNEAPOLIS, MN

Note to Librarians, Teachers, and Parents:

Blastoff! Readers are carefully developed by literacy experts and combine standards-based content with developmentally appropriate text.

Level 1 provides the most support through repetition of high-frequency words, light text, predictable sentence patterns, and strong visual support.

Level 2 offers early readers a bit more challenge through varied simple sentences, increased text load, and less repetition of high-frequency words.

Level 3 advances early-fluent readers toward fluency through increased text and concept load, less reliance on visuals, longer sentences, and more literary language.

Level 4 builds reading stamina by providing more text per page, increased use of punctuation, greater variation in sentence patterns, and increasingly challenging vocabulary.

Level 5 encourages children to move from "learning to read" to "reading to learn" by providing even more text, varied writing styles, and less familiar topics.

Whichever book is right for your reader, Blastoff! Readers are the perfect books to build confidence and encourage a love of reading that will last a lifetime!

This edition first published in 2011 by Bellwether Media, Inc.

No part of this publication may be reproduced in whole or in part without written permission of the publisher. For information regarding permission, write to Bellwether Media, Inc., Attention: Permissions Department, 5357 Penn Avenue South, Minneapolis, MN 55419.

Library of Congress Cataloging-in-Publication Data
Green, Emily K., 1966–
  Foxes / by Emily Green.
    p. cm. – (Blastoff! readers: Backyard wildlife)
  Includes bibliographical references and index.
  Summary: "Developed by literacy experts for students in kindergarten through grade three, this book introduces foxes to young readers through leveled text and related photos"–Provided by publisher.
  ISBN 978-1-60014-441-7 (hardcover : alk. paper)
  1. Foxes–Juvenile literature. I. Title.
  QL737.C22G7246 2010
  599.775–dc22   2010006432

Printed in the United States of America, North Mankato, MN.
080110   1162

Contents

A fox is a type of **wild** dog.

Foxes have thick fur. They have red, black, white, tan, or gray fur.

Foxes have bushy tails. A fox's tail is a warm cover in cold weather.

Some foxes
have white tips
on their tails.

Foxes live in lots of places. Many live in forests and **farmlands**.

Most foxes sleep
during the day.
They hunt for
food at night.

Foxes eat **insects**, grass, and fruits. Sometimes they bury food to eat later.

Foxes are great hunters. They catch mice, birds, rabbits, and snakes.

Foxes wait quietly for animals to come by. Then they **pounce**!

Glossary

farmlands—lands that are used for growing crops or raising animals

insects—small animals with six legs and hard outer bodies; insect bodies are divided into three parts.

pounce—to jump on something and grab hold of it

wild—living in nature

To Learn More

AT THE LIBRARY

Aylesworth, Jim. *The Tale of Tricky Fox*. New York, N.Y.: Scholastic, 2001.

Banks, Kate. *Fox*. New York, N.Y.: Farrar, Straus and Giroux, 2007.

Bunting, Eve. *Red Fox Running*. New York, N.Y.: Clarion Books, 1993.

ON THE WEB

Learning more about foxes is as easy as 1, 2, 3.

1. Go to www.factsurfer.com.

2. Enter "foxes" into the search box.

3. Click the "Surf" button and you will see a list of related Web sites.

With factsurfer.com, finding more information is just a click away.

Index